THE FOCUS OF LIFE
AUSTIN OSMAN SPARE

THE FOCUS OF LIFE

AUSTIN OSMAN SPARE

DEDICATED
TO
L.C.O'C.S.
"*vestigia nulla retrorsum*"

II

THE MUTTERINGS OF AĀOS

APHORISM I

" The effort of remembering
in the Valley of Fear."

KI.A OF THE EFFIGIES SPEAKS OF ZOS IN SOLILOQUY:

 BRING A SWORD THAT CONTAINS ITS OWN MEDICINE: THE SOUR MILK THAT CURETH THE BODY. PREPARE TO MEET GOD, THE OMNIFARIOUS BELIEVING, - *THYSELF THE LIVING TRUTH.*

Die not to spare, but that the world may perish.
Nature is more atrocious. Learning all things from *Thee* in
the most sinister way for representation: from thy thought to
become thereafter.
Having suffered pleasure and pain, gladly dost thou deny the
things of existence for freedom from desire --
mess of inequality - once so desired.
And is fear ofdesire. The addition to the 'I' ofa greater illusion.
Desire is the conception I and induces Thou.
There is neither thou nor I nor a third person - loosing this
consciousness by unity of I and Self; there would be no limit
to consciousness in sexuality.
Isolation in ecstasy, the final inducement, is enough - But,
procreate thou alone!
Speak not to serve but to scoff. Hearest thou, heaven's loud
guffaw?
Directly the mouth opens it speaks *righteousness.*
In the ecstatic laughter of men I hear their volition towards
release.
How can I speak that for which I have necessitated silence?
Salvation shall be *Unsay all things:* and true, as is time, that
speaketh all things.
Of what use are hints or stage whispers?
True wisdom cannot be expressed by articulate sounds.
The language of fools - is words.
In the labyrinth of the alphabet the truth is hidden.
It is one thing repeated many times.
Confined within the limits or rationalism; no guess has yet
answered.

o Zos, thou art fallen into the involuntary accident of birth and rebirth into the incarnating ideas of women.

A partial sexuality entangled in the morass of sensual law. On earth the circle was fabricated.

The origin of *all* things is the complex self. How shall it be made the end of things?

Dubious of all- things by this increase, and ignorance of individuality.

I or Self, in conflict, separate.

This forgetfulness of symboli becomes the unexplored 'reason' of existence.

Unable to conceive the events of the present: what shall be knowledge of past and future? Verily, this creator speaks 'I know not what I do.'

And in this living nightmare, where *all* is cannibalism. Why dost thou deny thyself? Verily, Man resembles his creator, in that he consumes himself in much filth.

Heaven gives indiscriminately of its superabundance to make the ghastly struggle called existence.

The necessity was a deliberate serving of its own pleasure becoming

more alien. Remoteness from self is pain and

precocious creation.

Through this remoteness from Self- thou dost not hear thine own call to be potentially Thyself. The living Self does not habitate.

There is no truth in thy wish. Pleasure wearies of thee.

Ecstatic fulfilment of ecstasy, is it asking too much?

Alas, the smallness of man's desire!

Thou too shalt suffer all things once again: unimagined sensations, and so consume the whole world.

o Zos, thou shalt live in millions of forms and every conceivable thing shall happen unto Thee.

Remember these senses are that which thou hast desired.

What is all thought but a morality of the senses that has become sex?

What is desired of the Self is given - eventually.

The *desire* is sufficient. The 'Self,' *will* pleasure in all things.

There is only one sense, - the sexual. There is only one desire, - procreation.

I am the cause - thou the effect.
I am all that I conceive. Not for all time but at some time.
'I multiply I' is creation: The sexual infinity.
There is no end to the details of my extreme likeness.
The more chaotic - the more complete am I.
The soul is the ancestral animals. The body is their knowledge.
This omnivorous soul, how lusty: it would seem to be
everlasting in its suicide.
These modified sexualities are the index of knowledge; this
realized; the dualities do not obstruct with associations that
involve infinite complexities and much education.
Existence is a continuation of self~realization.To create value
where there is none. By all desire being *one* there is no
overlapping nor the later necessity of undesiring. Complex
desire is the further creation of different desire, not the
realization of (particular) desire.
o Zos, Thou shall die of extreme youth! Death is a disease of
fear.
All is a backward walking - realized incapacity of volition:
To walk towards thyself.
With thine infinite self multiplication of associations Thou
knowest all things.
Among sentient creatures human birth is highly desirable,
man desires emancipation - liberation to his primeval self.
Remember! Didst thou leave the high estate for worse things?
Man becomes what he relapses into.
Cast into demoniacal moulds, human nature is the worst
possible nature.
The degenerate need women, dispense with that part of
thyself.
Give unto her all thy weaknesses, it is the suffering half.
Pain awaits him, who is sentimentally desirous.
Be it thus: 'Woman, there shall be no vintage from our kisses'.
In man and woman is thy 'being.' But I say, Thou could'st
create this body anew.
Awake! The time has come for the new sexualities!
Then would be occasion for greater pleasures.
To improve the species ye men must love one another.
This old illusion of righteousness has gained a future state
wherein men labour every doubt.

Thou art that which thou dost prefer. The seer, the instrument of seeing, or the seen.

Conscious desire is the negation of possession: the procrastination of reality.

Make thy desire subconscious; the organic is creative impulse to will.

Beware of thy desire. Let it be something that implies nothing but itself.

There are no differences - only degrees of sensation.

Provoke consciousness in touch, ecstasy in vision.

Let thy highest virtue be: "Insatiety of desire, brave self, indulgence and primeval sexualism."

Realization is not by the mere utterance of the words 'I am l' nor by self-abuse, but by the living act.

If the desire for realization exists in thee, sensuous objects will continually provide conveniences.

Realization of this Self, which is all pleasure at will, is by consciousness of one thing in belief. To be the same is the difficulty.

Thought is the negation of knowledge. Be thy business with action only. Purge thyself of belief: live like a tree walking!

Take no thought of good or eviL Become self,active causality by Unity of thine, I and Self.

Reality exists but not in consciousness of such: this phenomenal'!' is noumenal and neither,neither.

Now thus is concentration explained: "The will, the desire, the belief; lived as inseparable, become realization."

Truth concerns exactitude of belief, not reality.

He who has no law *is* free. In all things there is no necessity. Become weary of devising wisdom in morals.

Many unseemly words have been spoken in self slander, what more painful than that? For in the mud I tread on thee. The path men take from every side is mine.

There is nothing more to be said.

'I' - infinite space.

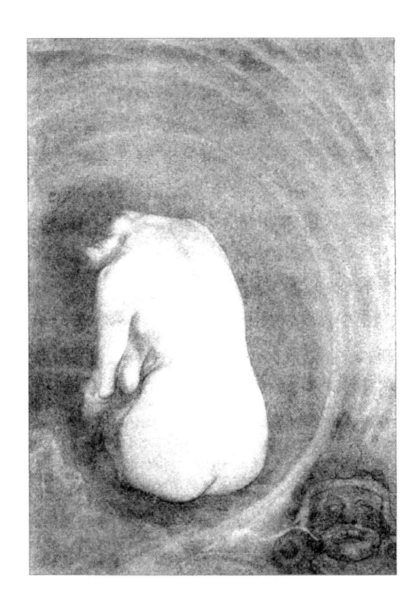

APHORISM II

"Morals of shadow,
wherein the Arcana of Zos
has no commandments"

ZOS SPEAKS OF IKKAH:

EAVING ASIDE ALL UNREAL DREAMS, CONSIDER THIS WORLD AS INSINCERE DISBELIEF. LO THIS DAY SALVATION HAS COME. MY 'I AND SELF' HAS AGREED IN BELIEF.

I would ask of thee thy *suppressed* self. Is it not the new thing desired?

No man shall follow me. I am not thy preservation. *Thou art the way.*

Assuredly, thy virtue is to be equally different.

Thy complaint is the calamity: The hypocrite is always at prayer.

Dost thou suffer? Thou shalt *again* suffer, till thine I does not fear its body. Rather seek and increase thy temptations, it is but the way to intelligence.

Transgression is wiser than prayer: Make this thy obsession. Thank only thyself and be silent.

The coward's way is religion. There is no fear - but righteousness.

Let this be thy one excuse, *I pleasured myself.*

Brave laughter - not faith. Rewarded are the courageous for they *shall pass!*

Thine I is envious of satisfaction. Yet none devotes himself to reality.

Whoever leameth much, unleameth all sentimental and *small* desires.

This is the new atavism I would teach: Demand of God equality - usurp!

The mighty are righteous for their morals are arbitrary.

Live beyond thought in courageous originality.

These hopes and fears are somnism, there is little reality.

Repent not, but strive to sin in *thine* own way, *light-heartedly:* without self~reproach. One becomes the thing itself or its creature.

Judge without mercy, all this weakness is thy self-abuse.

Experience is by cOntract. The great experience: Seduce thyself to pleasure.

There is only one sin - suffering.

There is only one virtue - the will to self~pleasure.

The greatest - the greatest non-morally.

The origin of morality is obedience to the earliest form of government.

In youth, all things *have* to obey their parents.

O, my aged IKKAH, loose this the navel cord, that my youth may pass!

The most important outcome of human effort is that we learn to become righteous thieves: To possess more easily of others for self-advantage.

In this incessant glorification of work, I discover a great human secret: "Do *thou* the work - I my pleasure."

As above so below, this is never sufficiently realized .

. . . Remorse? Nay, do unto thyself all things, *fearlessly.*

Finality is reached when ye have learned to digest everything.

What is all man-slaughter but what ye have done unto yourself?

Only where there is necessity is there death. Dispense with all '*means*' to an end.

There is nothing higher than joyous sensation.

Eternal Self! these millions of bodies 1 have outworn!

Oh, sinister ecstasy. 1 am thy vicious self pleasure that *destroyeth all things.*

Distrust thy teacher, for 'divine truth' has prevented better men from wisdom. In such revelation there is no *suggestion.*

Do thy utmost unto others: But be surely what thou wilt: *and* keep thy belief free of morality.

Observe thyself by sensation: thus know the finer perturbations

and vibrations.

This much shalt thou learn: To love *all* men, for there will be compulsion.

Serve no man, hell is a democracy.

Think not the words 'I wish,' say not the words 'I will.'

Respect thy body: it will again become thy parents.

Fear nothing, - *strike* at the highest.

Ennui is fear: Death is failure. Go where thou fearest most.

How canst thou become great among men? ... *Cast thyself forth!* Of this event, genius is the successful effort of memory.

Break *thy* commandments, be lawless unto *all* dogma.

Revolt is the fertiliser of the new faculties.

Knowledge and all evil wars react from previous existences that are now fragmentary to the body and operate as disembodied astrals.

The more distant the creature that govern our functions the more unusual is our manifestation of phenomena, which are but living their physical peculiarities by a mechanism.

Retrogress to the point where knowledge ceases, **in** that law becomes its own spontaneity and is freedom.

If my word has spoken unto fragments, pushed aside marriage beds, and brushed out old grave chambers;

If I ever rej oiced in calumnies, if I have murdered, lied, adulterated, robbed; **If** like the weather I spit on all thingsIs it because - I remember, that of my belief - *there is* a *volition that willeth opposite?*

For I love thee, O Self!

For I love thee, O mine I!

Oh! how could I fail to be agog for originality in self-love?

Never yet has procreation with another been satisfactory.

If I have wandered into marriage with *anything* - there has been a conspiracy of accidents: within and without.

And *what* willeth to self-pleasure - this out-breather ofgood taste, this conversion to ungodliness?

I know thee! ... thou heavenly necessity that compelleth chance *to supersede the sexualities!*

For mine I is worthy of the Self: and alone knows what is righteousness.

Verily, I tell you good and evil are one and the same.

It is but the distance *thou* hast reached.

Will unto self,love - the unexhausted, the procreative of ecstasy!

Where there is life there is will unto pleasure - however paradoxical the manifestation.

Where living things command they risk nothing but their own law.

I am *whatever* must surpass conceivable desire.

This Self,love does not circumscribe nor promise but gives whatsoever is taken - spontaneously.

Thus I teach thee, will unto pleasure of *all* things, for they must again change the tenacity to obedience.

And this new name I give unto thee, for all accusations: Not sinner, but somnambulist.

For he who premeditates, acts in his sleep.

Having overcome the difficulty of obtaining a male incarnation from parents not too venereal, one's habitation should be wandering among men: Employment, devotion to Art: Bed, a hard surface: Clothes of camel hair: Diet, sour milk and roots of the earth. All morality and love of women should be ignored. To whom does not such abandonment give the unknown pleasure?

Again I say: 'In all things' pleasure Thyself, for occasion need not be.

APHORISM III

"The Chaos of the Normal"

IKKAH SPEAKS OF HIMSELF:

 WOULD COUNSEL CLOSED EARS, FOR THOSE WHO CONTAIN THE GREAT IDEAS, HAVE NO OPINIONS. WHO DOTH KNOW WHAT HIS OWN SUBCONSCIOUS--NESS CONTAINS? STILL LESS HIS OWN ARCANA?

They are the great who allow its operation by silence.
Of two things we have choice: degeneration or immobility.
Out of the past cometh this *new* thing.
Becoming heaven's slaves - is some of pleasure begged again?
Man strives for increase, - the monstrous world of vague
and mad Ideas is incarnating.
Come back, your goal is ajail! Tum aboutandyouarrive .....
This maddest of worlds. Daily is pleasure limited by the
necessity of cheapened facilities.
Onwards and ever more weary - till sleep - then backwards.
Th r is nothing conceivable that does not exist, *because* the
vision is feeble.
In keeping the right distance from Things, is Safety. But how
much should we gain?
Experience is ignorance. The necessity of reoccurrence.
One thing is certain: we are subject to our own moral laws,
whether we are or are not aware of them.
The desire determines, and no later belief shall alter it a whit.
The highest creations are those that harmonize the most
incongruous things.
Art is the truth we have realized of our belief.
The great human factor in Life is deceit: Always the greater
deceiver - self? The wrath is revealed against all that hold
the truth in righteousness.

Still are the shallownesses, who could know they hide a universe?

And tell me, what is it the obvious does not contain?

Know much of life! Should death give *you* its secret?

Self suggestion - *to will,* this is the great teacher: not dogma.

To those of fixed Ideas, beware of suppressed evacuation.

What the world reveres most, treat with the utmost contempt.

Consumption, evacuation, sleep: this labour suffers of no variation for to~morrow we again procreate life.

O, fool! suicide does not exist ... there is no death.

Death is change and for many very *small* change.

You who stink like a butcher's shambles - what is your daily menu?

Become less cai"Ilivorous. If the food is wholesome, the body shall not suffer.

The difference between man and beast is one of acquisition, not digestion.

There is no lasting peace - ye eternally fall in love with the new thing of belief.

To the mental gymnast: your somersault returns from the place where it began.

Slave! All you know for certain - *you suffer.*

Embrace reality by imagination.

From birth is a degeneration of function - safe is he who never leaves his mother's womb.

What is perfect does not reflect its caricature. What is true has no argument - in that it is volition.

The workers of *malignity* own the Kingdom of Earth.

What asses these teachers, prophets and moralists now appear!

And through them what greater she-asses we have become!

You would have prophecy? First tell me your sleeping partner's name ...

What once evoked a mighty passion - is now repulsive; lest ye forget: sleep alone.

Ifyou yourselfcannot be ungodly - then nothing will convert you.

No nearer the goal for life is eternal.

Which are more unclean: they who make a profession of their morality, or they who prostitute?

Life is a viscous charity from which germinates friendships

towards parasites.

The necessity of a better life is intoxication but more and greater things than strong drink intoxicate.

Thou hast become remote - I rejoice in thee!

Who invented such things as vanity and humiliation?

The higher the form of creation the more it habitates earth and the more it is conscious of body.

Everything that is half realized becomes the material of dreams; man has always badly mixed the dream with the reality.

He who transcends time escapes necessity.

The living Lord speaks: 'In disciples is my satisfaction.' A weary one asked: 'Is it not written on the sandals of the prostitute - *follow* me '?

All undesirable things become morally fearsome.

Only the animal in man dances ...

Hatred is life - the love of possession.

He who can truthfully say - I believe in nothing but myself - in all things realized.

HE ABYSS SELF PROJECTING FROM NON-EXISTENCE THE PROCREATRIX I, WAS THE GREAT CHANGE AND THE BEGINNING: TO EXTEND THE PURPOSE OF DESIRE - FOR TIME TO MAKE ALL EXISTENCE INEXACT -

Those things kept ever vague.
Thus was the *will* to operate unbegotten.
One thing nominally, everything alternatingly desirous. That which is first desired is permitted, then externalized and taken away by a circumlocution of beliefs becoming law.
No knowledge would separate us from the virtues of nonexistence
but that for man - having become involved with
disease, all his food is poisonous; his complete saturation is inevitable that he may become again healthy. Thus man wills by thought.
By the 'death posture"[1] (not for subjection of mind, body or longevity nor any *thmgas* such) the Body is allowed to manifest spontaneously and is arbitrary and impervious to reaction.
Only he who is unconscious ofhis actions has courage beyond good and evil: and is pure in this wisdom of sound sleep.
Will to pleasure is the basic function underlying all activity whether conscious or not, - and whatsoever the means.
Denial of this Self-love is disease - the cause of homicide;
the sufferings ofpart-sexualities and small things germinating.
Knowledge of necessities is desirous: - Deliberation is but a sorry dissatisfaction - a first cause of illusions, harnessing
man to a mass of half-realized desires. Remember! o Ikkah, these present Ideas of consciousness obtaining in senses and bodies, are transitory - are destined for *usage* and other

---

[1] A simulation of death by the utter negation of thought, i.e. the prevention of desire from belief and the functioning of all consciousness through the sexuality.

predeterminations - and unnecessary to wakefulness. Will is transition; the painful process of transmigration - the labour of birth of death. Volition to supersede a thing is inability to realize the living Self. For whatever is attained is but the re-awaking of an earlier experience of body.

Man should most desire a simultaneous consciousness of his separate entities. All consciousness of 'I' is a decline and vegetates good and evil afresh - the compulsion of limit and morality. From spontaneous non-existence, germinate all significant ecstasy - that shall last in the uttermost impossibilities unconditioned to will.

Alas! what ornaments are grave-yards? The pleasure ground of self is contact with the living.

The fool hastens to man with a mouth overfull of new discoveries of power subservient to will! What matters it that we have realized a little more of I? Of beyond its limits of possibility?

Note well! *All* things are possible even in nightmares becoming, they are a necessity, an additional boundary to memory - the further separate entities of consciousness. Remember O Ikkah! Thou shall not cease to be again what is denied - unto the end of conception: thus man has constructed his seed. These sentient creatures and the beyond conceptions in the order of evolution were thou once even as they?

O Ikkah, Thou art this present God - this termite and many other things not yet domesticated or associated with thought. This focus 'I' called consciousness is unaware of its entire living embodiments but alternates and epitomizes their personalities. What is 'I' and the extent of its conscious habitation?

... A weak desire, a memory governed by ethics and ignorant of its own bodies. Therefore that which is indeliberate is the more vital and is will: discarded knowledge is the sexuality and becomes law.

Thus entity exists in many units simultaneously without consciousness of 'Ego' as one flesh. Verily, I say - the deliberations of many exist in living animations - their consciousness split among a multitude of creatures but knowing only the more important (?) incarnations - 'What greater misery than this?

Of others, their awake-consciousness is aware of more than one entity and obtain ecstasy by saturable desire.

o Ikkah! Jest viciously! Abandon this haunted mortuary in a blind turning - by significant courage.

The 'I' surfeit-swelled is the end ofcompassion - the indrawing ofsex to Self,love. Fortunate is he who absorbs his female bod, ies - ever projecting - for he acquires the extent of his body. Whatever is desired, predetermines its existence in endless ramifications miserably and evanescent: Self,love is the para, dox *of!*.

Oh Ikkah Zod,ka! Thy fiction of finality has prevented sleep and created eternity. O, invent *sound sleep* by the utter ruin of cosmos!

For impalpably and anterior to consciousness - all things exist ...

With sensibility and name, becoming its living simulation and thus it disappears - involving its consequent necessity. Reason has become too sensible, thus desire has become legerdemain mixed with diablerie. The soul, proud and blighted ... is a civil war of desire: thereof the necessity for medicine and anesthesia. Man has made this environment: the mind is now the belly of the sexuality. Thus I suggest to thee - Self,love and its own temptation to excess.

Verily, greater courage hath none than to satisfy the *unexpected* desire by Self,pleasure.

For this reason, that when the desire again reacts, to operate in the ego, the suffering shall be *ecstatic.* How do I know? Not by farcical dialogue with Self but through contact with its undulations ... are we not ever standing on our own volcano? What is beyond man - somethingmore dishonest or a further beast?

One thing is desired, another is thought; and a *different* becomes.

Everything loved obtains an obscene disease. These dream postures are ominous prophecy of thyself to become - the obscure wish. O joy and woe! which is the higher moralityto love man while being man or to reincarnate as woman to fulfil desire? Death is that degeneration, an alternation ofego in consciousness (*i. e.,* desire), its metamorphosis into separate entities for that purpose: serving its own. Man's living virtues

are those unfamiliar with names. His absurd I is ever supralapsarian. Manhas exhausted his courage by imaginations engendered from the damned: Never can he satisfy what follows these repressions.

Thou who tremblest all over! Thy soul shudders! Thou dost perish from the poison of yesterday's amour and righteousness! o incomprehensible synonymy! O thou who art neither the vigorous kiss ofmy twin sexes nor its writhings of hatred and black shame. Nothing is discovered of thee until *I* invented it: from the ceaseless resurrection of earlier deliberations. O thou syzygy of my I and Self! Thou becomest volatile to whatsoever is sensed. Art thou the hidden wish for madness and hysteric love? O thou "untamed" within, thou shall not lose virtue - for *thee* I will not domesticate while generating. o Idiocy! where is that path where I may wander naked in frenzy, a trespasser against all things reasonable? O time! saith good and evil: 'Corne, corne! Ego, I corne!'

Knowledge alone is transitory, the illusion subsequent to 'I desire all things.'

Eternal, without beginning is Selfj without end am I; there is no other power and substance. The ever changing modifications and diversities we see are the results of forgetfulness, misinterpretated by nightmare senses. When the Self again desires, then *I* only and nothing else shall remain. Permitting all things, whatsoever is imagined comes out of it. Believe what you will, it has no compassion. The connotation Self~love is applicable to all things. To it, all things are equal. The destroyer of *devotees;* lover of all things *unique.*

Giving overflow to all who are indifferent to wanglers, who jest at doctrines ... of emancipation in celibacy and vituperation. I declare this Self~pleasure alone is free of Theism; the disenthralment of God and the distractions of ego in the many entities of existence I show.

Ye who praise Truth thereby causing its necessity are compelled to live differently. Out of this afterthought of belief- thrives this somnambulating generation ofunpleasured fools, liars and homicides - everbewildered by good and evil. All has become inborn sex, so complex 'am I,' that a successful awakening is impossible without catastrophe. Birth is now painful, life a dire necessity and death an uncertainty - except of fearsome things. What further, O Ikkah, should a cesspool of truths contain? Nor truth, nor women, nor *anything* else once made objective shall satisfy. They who are committed to doctrines shall continue to move in this cycle of transmigrating belief: degenerating beyond limits they dare not face, and so allow conception to exist *ofitselffrom* the imaginations 'I believe.' What more disgusting? For I am all sex. What *I* am *not* is moral thought, simulating and separating. Imagined through forgetfulness, born asleep, whose very essence is vague, how can this world with such vapid antecedents, be anything but unthinkable! What man prohibits and then commits will certainly cause suffering, because he has willed double. Born of complex desire, results of actions are dual: multitudinous virtue and vice. Creation is caused through this formula of reaction and is a servile believing, - all this universe has come out of it. When by that unprohibiting SelHove all this cosmos is certainly familiar and pleasured, it should be practised with labour.

But who is honest enough to believe this without relapse? Having renounced both good and evil conveniently, one should engage in spasmodic madness. Renouncing everything else take shelter in that Self-Iove,which incites the functions into the bold, 'freedom from necessity am 1': virtue and vice shall cease. Self-illumination am I; the procreatrix of this universe. Indomitable in body: born of the bastard truth I made. When the eyes are shut the world certainly does not exist. O chaos! is there no greater joy than flagellation; the ecstatic paralysis that makes holocausts of withered souls; the hideously pitiable cripples - "I fear ... "? I assert this Self~ love to be a most secret ritual hidden by blasphemous Ideographs: and he who calls, pronouncing the word fearlessly, the entire creation of women shall rush into him.

What are lies - but mistimed events?
What is time but a variety of one thing?
What is all folly, but will?
What are all beliefs but the possibilities of I?
What is all future but resurrection?
What is all creation but thyself?
Why is all existence? Awake! Up! up, for thine own sakeSelf~ love discover.

O sin, where is thy violence?
O love, where is thine incest?
O thought, where is thy courage?
O hope, where is thy faith?
O Self where is thy humanity?
O truth, where is thy mispronunciation?
Verily, Self~love alone is complete!

THE SEXUALITY

AND

SLEEP OF AĀOS

 AOS HAVING REALIZED AT AN EARLY AGE THAT ALL SYSTEMS OF BELIEF, RELIGION AND RITUALS; CONSISTED ALONE IN THEIR ORIGINAL VALUE TO THEIR CREATORS; AND WERE OF THE WEARY, TO incarnate pleasure by hope, control by fear; and to *Deify* by morals;

That cowards fear, and must needs promise pleasure of their sufferings; And they who had experienced "I," would have you destroy its body; and were but outspoken hypocrites their manifestation of pleasure being *potential:* Verily, Aaos realized that the origin of **I,** was for pleasurable procreation ... but that things had been changed.

Aaos then pondered in his heart long over the geometry of the world of senses; and spake thus: "How far short has reali~ zation fallen from original conception? Have we not lived all things previous to the event? What is *any* desire but all de~ sire? but men get married and nothing is sufficiently arbitrary. I am the origin of all creation, certain it is that *I* want not salvation, (observing all the miserably diseased mob:)

"O, grant that I may add to the world a far greater suffering! God is a precocious creation of the Apes, something that must be suppressed: Man must regain his sexuality.

What is man - this feeder on dead bodies of Self? . . . A mole, a carnivorous plant, a disease of himself, a conglomeration of - "it was" and a cause, effecting the miscarriage ofhis desires - ever creating his future necessities:

What man knoweth the perturbations of his own fear?
Verily, suffering is its own reward.

He who *willed,* knoweth not his own offspring.

Man projects a vague 'Self' and calls it truth and many other
qualified names: Verily, once a Thing is named it becomes
nothingness to its meaning.

All happiness is an illusion and a sorry snare. All righteousness
is a dishonesty and all sin a pleasure. Assuredly, the courageous
alone seem safe ... without remorse.

Man invented Self;pleasure but knoweth not his own love.
Everything was once arbitrary. Yet they who spoke: theirpower
has ended in common sexual practice - abnormal only with
jaded appetites. They who knewwere rightly crucified, scorned,
ignored and their mouths sealed with their own excrement.
Have we not forgotten more than we shall ever learn?
Where is the magic to revitalize the mouldering words?
Everything is again eventually arbitrary!

What is there to believe that is free of belief? What is there to
will that is safe from reaction?

Why is belief always incarnating? Though oft times not even
a sincere wish? Who among men knoweth what he believes?
Everything is true at some time.

What is this unpleasant Thing, necessity - suffering? How
originated pain? What is necessity - but conditioned belief?
What is it we eternally desire and say, *through* disease?
Verily, directly a man speaketh - he suffers.

What is Self and I? And all these myriad forms called creation,
- all so essentially like me? Who can realize this Selr
portraiture of all Things?

Verily, the sexuality has no limit in conception.
Whither I would go, there had I long been before.

Eternal re~occurence would seem necessary to greater multiplicity!

For what reason is this loss of memory by these bewilding refractions of my original image, - that *I once made* - and out of which spring the sexes?

God is born again of desire, call it by whatever name: this unmanifested memory has no name till belief incarnates. Hence it may be called, - *the re-occuring sub-division* of T. Everything becomes necessary.

Man is subject to his own law: All else is an obscene jest and a lie."

Thus reasoned Aaos in his youth and went to sleep alone. After a vilely repulsive nightmare Aaos awoke saying: "Quiescent are my depths, who could realize They contain such criminal abortions of the cosmos?"

What is all b,ody but materialized desire? What are dreams but unsatisfied desires striving to foretell their possibility in despite of morals?

Life is but will, that has become organic after satiety; its further desires striving for Unity. Death is that further will incarnating in body."

The next day Aaos spoke unto his growing beard: "Destroy O, my Self, these hallucinations of *I* am *not* by knowledge of pleasure.

Thou mighty ecstasy that willeth *Thy* pleasure in suffering! Make my consciousness reality of thee in body!

What is Self but Cosmos? What is I but Chaos? Eternally creating its pleasure, everything *could* become arbitrary. Whatever deceit we practice, the functions of the emotions are one; their expression dual: Time making multitudinous by denial.

What is experience, but denial? What is the centre, but belief?"
After a long suspiration, Aaos spoke aloud to his'!':
"Awake, my Self,love! Leave this hour of cow,dust, I am all
things to pleasure. Too long have I lived the nightmares of
others in my sleep ... Arise! get forth and feed from the
mighty udder of Life.

Thou art not a cow,herd, nor grass, neither cows nor kine!
But once again, a creator of cows - who loves their breasts!
Are not all things cows to thy pleasure - whether they would
or not?

And what is Cow? Is it not a fountain? Didst thou not create
God, teach nature all secrets and crowd the spaces with cows
of desire, unknown and manifesting? Didst thou not create
and *destroy Woman?*"

Again Aaos spoke, but unto his lidless eye:

"Behold thou hoary, white headed, thou silent watcher ofnight
and day: thou death~clutchon the smallnesses of Time!
This neither~neither I, shall transvalue ennui, fear, and all
diseases to my wish. Dead is my misery in suffering! How could
it exist in my Zodiac, unwilled? I, who transcend ecstasy by
ecstasy meditating *Need not be* in Self~love! Verily, this
constant ecstasy I indraw from Self~creation. By castrating
'of,' my belief is balanced: my arbitrary automatism serving
its diverse self~pleasure."

Then Aaos meditated and murmured: "All things exist by
me: all men exist in me, yet who doth not turn away from his
own superabundance while realizing?

All desire is for unity: thus my vision seeth through mine
ears.

Let my unity be realized sufficiently, thus shall my sexuality
be convenient unto itself and escape the conceivable ...
Where is lust when the tests wither? Verily these senses have
a further purpose beyond their own: thus shall thou steal the

fire from Heaven. All things return to their earliest functions."
At that moment Aaos realized he was not alone; and a voice
asked: "Hast thou no fear?" Laughing aloud, Aaos answered:
"Hidden from thy small susceptibilities, monstrous enormities
are committed!

On the day my wind bloweth a little the cow~dustawaythou
O fool, shalt vomit hot blood at thine own prostitution
and incest.

When thou knowest not, the lust wills *non-rationally,* the belief
bindeth with modest Ideas; the body is subject and suffers.
What man can prevent his belief from incarnating? Who is
free of filth and disease?

All men are servile to the great unconsciousness of their
purpose in desire. The I thinks, the Self doth. There is no
salvation from desire, neither day nor night does it cease its
lengthy procreation ofcause and effect: penetrating all things
inexplicably.

Endless are its elements and nothing whatsoever escapes its
embrace - but its own Self,love. . .. hOlllcli fear my!?"
Alios lowering his voice, uttered: "What further use shall I
give my sexuality? Verily it is alway speaking for me!
This I, non,resisting to the Self, becomes irresistible." When
the voice had left, Alios went his way muttering and smiling:
"Can it be possible that dead wives resurrect?" For he thought
that - *Woman was dead.*

With this reflection Alios became silent. Awaking from his
Self,introspection he spake aloud to his body:

"Man is something that has resurrected from an archetype, a
previous desire gone to worms. All conceptions predetermine
their degeneration or supersedure by degrees of morality.
Verily a new sexuality shall be mine, - unnecessary to
degenerate or surpass.

To give it a name, I call it the *Unmodifled* sexuality; without a name it shall be conscious of all desire: thus no ecstasy shall escape me. Its wisdom shall be dreams of Self~love vibrating all the manifestations - *I am he, who self pleasures nonmorally."*

The dead body of *Aaos:*
Aaos preparing for death uttered **in** soliloque:
"O, thou inconceivableness that transcends human desire; thou magnificent incongruous Face. For millions of years thou hast not wearied of my body. What would Thy pleasure be but for my wantonness?"

"I teach you the glad death of all things." Thus spake my knowing mouth. "My belief has created the more beautiful body and desires rebirth.

Fear I the transvaluation called death? Knew I not death, when time was born? Arise, old memory! And tell my consciousness of this frequent experience - once again!"

Then Death spake unto Aaos:

"No stranger, nor enemy to me is Aaos, we are too ancient friends to come to blows. What hast thou come to take from me this time? What fresh associations for thy new body? No self~denial has Aaos! *Thou* hast not come to rap tables. To awake the disembodied Astrals!"

Aaos answered: "In my life my memory lived numerous remotenesses which were once me. My belief reached associations that out~stripped all morality and rationalism. My I chanced much with the Self: certain it is, I come not to repent ... nor seek a wife.

Yea, my will conquered faith and sincerely laughed at every righteousness!

Now that my individual consciousness dissolves, to saturate again with its furthermost desires, to form the new body: o mighty death, remember at the time of incarnating - my utmost immorality, my frightening madnesses, my jesting sins,

my satyr carouses, my grotesque concubine of chaos!
Remember O death, my frenzied longing that has no name
(Oh, forget my first kiss oflove, now withered as a fallen leaf).
Make this my sexuality complete, all knowing, so that I may
again procreate the lusty Self-love in isolation!"
Then Alios spake unto the ferryman:

"O time, of nothing now am I ashamed to admit parentage.
What I generate is future, body to become. I have learned
and unlearned in equal labouring this universe. Hard has been
my faith and denial. *That which is* incomprehensible have I
made, -have I impelled inwards to make secure for reaction.
My knowledge is but the murmuring of a few words with ever
changing intonation and meaning. For I have suffered that
which shall never be forgotten or spoken: Thus much have I
realized of Life. Where is fear when I impel procreation? O
earth! al1 memories! solid, liquid, vapour and flaming! Old
entiment is my body, germinating afresh: again to exist and
change by the command, 'I desire.' The Alpha and Omega of
my wisdom is - *glad suicide:* it has become inevitable and
shall be my payment to thee. Steel and poison are my friends.
Steel for Self, poison for vermin - for myself diseased. I *will*
this fruitful violence, my death kiss, thus to realize my hyper~
commands."

With his belieffirmly fixed, his full red lips smiling, with bright
eyes; Aaos clasped his sword saying: "Greater love hath no
man than Self-destruction in pleasure." No new experience
to Aaos! And thus he died.

DEATH is named the great unknown. Assuredly, death is the great *chance*. An adventure in will, that translates into body. What happens after death? Will it be more surprising than this world? Could I say ?My experience may not be the commonplace ... Without doubt, all shall experience the 'rushing winds' that blow from within, the body beyond perspective, into cosmic dust, - till consciousness again develops. Death is a transfiguration of life, an in~version, a reversion of the consciousness to parentage and may be a diversion! A continuation of evolution. The coming forth of the suppressed.

Do you know what happens to the body at death? Exactly what changes take place? Well, so it happens to your beliefs, desires, etc., that make consciousness, for all things seen are incarnate desire, the unseen; Ideas of the past and future bodies. From these the new body is determined and parentage selected by the laws of attraction.

The Death Posture

The wise man makes sure of *his future parents and* a *male incarnation before death.*

Consciousness (for most, only three dimensions) is not so definite as in life but to the extent of your will in life, that much is your consciousness in death.
Death is the manufacture of life. A dream is a sore likeness of Life.

Death is a sore dream of life. Its period depending on the

perfection or otherWise of the individual but closely follows in duration the previous life - till re,incarnation.

Death being a living nightmare of life, has painful possibilities - in the degree of unified consciousness. A ghostly world of 'perhaps' where all the vague potentialities of desire, are incarnating. There is no women as such.

Again I say, death is the great chance and there grasp where thou hast before failed in the body.

If fate is life, then death is the hazard to alter fate!

A world where will creates the *afterthought* in its own image. For most, death will hold mainly blank pages, but were we ever treated all alike?

Study your dreams in this life, it may help you in the death posture.

The heaven of Aaos:

"All things are subject to resurrection" thus spake smiling Aaos, on rising from the dead. Then turning towards his shadow .... "I come! the changing word that destroys religion, a vortex wind that shall jest in Temples!

Again! A reveller in the marshalled order of the sexes, the mad anarch of desires, the wild satyr of wolfish kisses! Once again to earth, O Thou whirlwind of desire, thou drunken breath of ribald lightning!

My vampire concubine of chaos, wound round the breasts of my being.

Drink of my chalice of ecstasy! Yea, as my rapacious flame reareth before thee, thou escapeth from me with the laughing whisper of thy wonderful pleasure!

O, LCO' CS!! thou insatiable thirst of my self~love, with none but thee will I procreate!

"%at*now*am I after resurrection? The sinful despair of magic? I am the Iconoclast ofLogos: The sun~satyrofChaos!Thunder and lightnings? Yea, a \;'ital gaiety to drowsy dust, to blase souls. Ecstatic laughter that reverberates and awakens ... I am the shuddering heights and suffocating depths of ego, slipping and becoming. Inconceivable women am 1. A clouded vista of abyss, wherein to visit naked, my vampire Self. Wherein to write a cryptic language of my sexes, that I am

the Key. Wherein to belch forth venomous atmosphere
towards the highest. Wherein to drench my thirsted tongue
on thy goat's milk; to battle with thy cataleptic kisses, to swoon
in thy consuming subtilty. O my mistress, I am unutterably
drunk striving thy depths. I am the great cypher of love and
hate knotted. The sphinx surviving, never sufficiently
imagined. I am the grotesque refractions of form and Self.
The bitter purgative, called death. A violence that out,lasts
the morning. Moon turbulent waters am I: the frightening
black Albatross of unashamed women - where men are. I
am the over mature breasts ofa child: the virgin womb, hidden
by nightmares. Constant in metamorphosis, permeating
creation without compassion. The unexcelled impulse that
has never failed. Yea, I am all these - yet never known. My
kiss is a sword thrust! For whom, am I, this insatiable fountain
in the hot deserts? Only for thee, O, L.C.O'CS!"
Thus sang Aaos, the blasphemer, throwing offhis grave shroud.
Going again among men (for he pleasured in *all* men), he
gave unto them his magic book, named: "Life and Death, the
jest called love, *wherein every man is a God, in whatsoever he
will his belief.*"
And *Aaos* passed *his* way, muttering to his goatish beard:

"What now is left all hope is dead? For I have buried my illusion
and dishonesty.
Thus my body is now all inconceivableness! O, God, where is
thine enemy?"

THE DREAMS
OF AĀOS

THE I

AND

THE ARCANUM

 NE DAY THE TIME DREW NEAR FOR THE EXPERIMENT AND AAOS WAS WATCHING THE WATERS, TO MAKE ARCANA BY ARBITRARY PROJECTION INTO THE UTTER VOID OF HIS ISOLATION. AND THIS WAS HIS WISH –

"in future my dreams shall interpretate themselves as will (*i.e.* reaction)."

For, he reasoned: "Why not live *asleep* all suffering?" Aaos had lived the preliminary ritual of habit in the cesspools and exhausted them in the mountains. Before projection he prayed thus to the waters: - "O thou I, vice versa - my God. I at least shall not be thy jest. In life I have realized possibilities not contained in heaven - amidst a cowardice inconceivable but accomplished everywhere. I have made known (opening his book) something that is different to the muck of retouched photography which men call reality: although it has been the evil habit of thousands of years.

I have created art (lived belief) that surpasses all evolved conception.

I have incarnated that which *I*- need to rationalize: Verily
- not the ever present portraiture of experience to satisfy
the ovine: No obvious allegory of asses - thinking God: No
still-life group ofempty bottles and old maids commonplaces:
Nor the gay-tragedy of song.

But strange desires of stranger arcana. The law I make while
thinking God - and will smash and remake again: *so that* I
may commit every conceivable sin against its word. My utility
has been - *my pleasure* - that alone is my service to man
and to heaven, in that I am the Goat."

After his devotion Aaos prepared for the Death posture and
judgement. Awaking from the awful wrath - his teeth
chattering, his limbs shivering and drenched with a cold
perspiration, he allowed the ague to exhaust itselfand thought
thus: "Verily, I have nothing to forgive or repent ... Alas!
what fears this Ibut its own conditions?

Man will create the faster moving body outside himself always
prefering compulsion to the infinite possibilities of
freedom.

Alas! Alas! that which is ornamental reacts its uselessnessthe
symbol '1 was.'

The necroloque of love - is utility. "Then rising from his
couch and taking an ecstatic inbreath: "Again would 1 die
violently and jest at God."

The operation having exhausted him he suffered this
daydream:

"The waters became murky, then muddy, and movement
began.

Going nearer, he observed - a phosphorescent morass
crowded with restless abortions of humanity and creatures like
struggling mudworms, aimless and blind: an immense

swamp of dissatisfaction; a desire smashed into pieces.
With his will, the dream changed and he became in a vast
warehouse-cum-brothel. Realizing his whereabouts he
muttered: "Such is life, an endless swallowing and procreation,
morally, man is a bastard."

The floor was strewn with dirty clothes and candle ends:
knowing the strangest women, nothing was pleasing enough
... so his attention wandered to the upper story. He was certain
he had been there before by a staircase. But now, there was
no easy means of access. He would have to climb whatever
served. After much painful effort he managed to reach and
hang on to the balustrade ofthe upper floor. There, he noticed
the tore contained innumerable strange effigies and new
creations of humanity. He struggled further along to obtain
an easy means of ingress, thinking: "Where there is desire there
shall be found the desired leeping partner. What is true,
is pleasurable Self. I have now reached the sixth letter of the
alphabet."When suddenly *he* observed another and more agile
following him -who when reaching Aaos, clutched hold of
him - shouting: "Where I cannot reach, thou too shall not
ascend." Their combined weight became too heavy - the
balustrading collapsed and they both fell ... Aa:os felt himself
falling as into a bottomless pit - when with a start he awoke,
and after introspection spoke to his heart: "Verily I have fallen
in love with a new belief and become moral! This I reflects
itself differently. What was once easy - is now difficult. All
reflections are radiated matter incarnating. Who doth know
what his own stillness refracts at the time of its projection?

Who would suspect afterthought without consciousness? The
I, to be self prophecy - without a conglomeration of old
clothes - is by a *deliberation previous to will-* to be noumenal;
is anterior to time. Forgive? (*i. e.* to free from consciousness).
Yea, a thousand times! so that the desire become large and
insane enough to *self-will.* How can memory forget - when
we invented reaction? What is all bad memory - but morality?
What is will but reaction - impulsed from the accidents of I?
Then Aaos remembered he had conditioned his realization
by thought oftime and remarked: "So ends in the *part* sexuality

53

- all asses' magic that premeditates time..Much thought
destroys the nerve. The arcana knows more than the I wills:
and thus should I have it."
Then Aaos laughed aloud and spoke: "Up! Up! my sexuality!
and be a light unto all- that is in me!"
For he had - while contemplating - eluded his I and knew
he would shortly obtain ... And thus he found a new use for
his righteousness.

SELF-LOVE

AND

MAP MAKING

 AOS IN HIS YOUTH HAD MANY DREAMS, PLEASING AND OTHERWISE; AWAKE AND IN HIS SLEEP. FREQUENTLY, FRAGMENTS OF DREAMS HAUNTED HIM FOR MANY A DAY, BUT *THEY* WERE OF HIS MARRIAGE

bed. After his divorce he slept alone with his sword. Aaos, once dreamed he was still asleep, and this was his dream: "He had been exploring an unknown country and having returned, was busy making maps from his rough sketches and memoranda. He was surprised how fresh was his memory of every questioned detail, at the ease with which his hand drew the mountains and contours of that unknown country. His dexterity became too pleasing and threatened an event long ceased and then forgotten. By his determination he awoke and was able to calm the excited passion. He was consoled that nothing had happened. Then he spoke to himself thus: "What new deceit is this? Must I be for ever solving the changing symbolism of the wretched morality - called "I"? Do *I* still need a loin cloth for my passions? Verily, to be alone and map drawing is now an unsafe art! Sleep? - This sexual excitement still obtains. Procreation is with more things than women. The function of the sexuality is not entirely procreation: stranger experiences are promised than ever imagination conceived! One must retain - to give birth to will. Behold! my Self-love, thee I pleasure too well, - to let slip into other being!"

AĀOS
AND THE
UNDERTAKER

NE DARK NIGHT, LEAVING THE TAVERN MORE OR LESS SOBER AND WANDERING WITHOUT THOUGHT, I ARRIVED AT A WELL ILLUMINATED UNDERTAKER'S SHOP. INTOXICATED, I AM ALWAYS CURIOUS OF THE WORK IN SUCH PLACES - SO HERE I PAUSED.

At that moment, the door was flung violently open and five drunken undertaker's assistants lurched into me. I objected in a mild way, they being numerous and I thinking that drunkards are lucky . . . But that any resistance or excuses I might offer would be unsatisfactory was too apparent. They had reached the quarrelsome state and I discovered - I knew these men too well! From argument to foul accusations (and what did they not call me?) - came blows - I thought it safer not to run away. Did I fight well? I know *they* did and with drunken humourdragged me into the shop to purchase a coffin. Within, came recognition -- Alas, too truly they knew me! From then no quarter was 'given. That drunken fight among the dead and funeral furniture was hopeless for me.
I was robbed, stripped, spat upon, kicked and bound - what abuse did I not suffer? I think the humiliation and blows rendered me unconscious!

But, I was not to rest so easily - they soon brought me back to consciousness for worse things ... And I was told they had recently finished making my wife's coffin. They then forced me to view her dead body. Even in my pitiable state, I thought of the beauty ofher corpse. Again, they reviled me because of her: she who, if I had not neglected her, would still be living. **I**, the whoremonger, betrayer ofwomen, and arch~abnormalist. After much other insult; they told me -myfate. I was given the choice of being burnt to death or buried alive with *her!* Naturally my choice was to be alone. But no such chance was to be mine. I was buried alive with her corpse. With their combined weight forcing on the lid. I thought I was dead (for did I not hear the rushing winds?) when doubt crept into my soul. Then realization of life dawned when I felt that cold corpse crushed against my body by the tightness of the coffin, - never have I realized such horror! With a mighty yell, my after suspiration burst that overcrowded coffin into fragments! I arose, thinking I was alone. But no, sitting by the corpse, amid the debris was - the *devil* grinning!

To be alone and half alive with the devil is not a welcome anti~climax ... Then he spoke unto me: "Coward! where was thy courage, even against drunken enemies? Ah ah! Thou hast indeed willed pleasure! Who has the power, Thou or I? What medicine for the dead Gods! Thou wretched scum of littlenesses - heal thy gaping wounds, thou art more fitted to pray than to prey." Much more did he utter, till my very ears closed. With a body torn to pieces, crushed in every part - what was I to answer? My silence compelled him again to speak: "Hast thou no complaint?" In a mighty rage - for this was a worse goad than all my earlier suffering - I answered: "Curses, no! keep your possessions. - *I will pleasure.* Do your utmost! this poor thing my body you will again replace! Then I fought the devil and behold, - I became alone!
What happened? I, in my miserable plight, not even my teeth left - how could I have conquered the devil? Did I become a succubus? Perhaps - I became the devil? But this I knowI did *will pleasure.*

And from this day shall smile in all men's faces.
Then Aaos awoke and murmured: "Belief and desire are the great duality which engender all illusions that entangle the senses (*i.e.* sexuality) and prevent *free* will. What is all accidental suffering but reaction from dead loves now become diableries.

How much are we sensible of body? Yet the composition of the body is its relationship between consciousness and all

creation.
Without doubt I am now an - undertaker!"

THE DEATH
OF
TZULA

N HIS SLEEP AAOS ONE DAY MET HIS SISTER TZULA AND LEARNED SHE WAS THINKING OF MARRIAGE AND SHE QUESTIONED HIM THUS: "MY MOST LOVED BROTHER, WHAT IS YOUR OPINION OF MY ENTERING MARRIAGE?

I would be guided by your experience and cunning on sexual matters. My body is weak from desire and suffers a horrible restlessness that surprises my habits of virginity." Aaos answered: "What cause is there for astonishment? This life force acts and invents from itself; *even* when the usual channels of expression are open. How much more so - when closed and the nature non,moral? With deceivers, one may well promise and not fulfil for this end, that with a *double will* there shall be satisfaction without the labour of birth. Resist not desire by repression: but transmute desire by changing to the greater object."

Tzula answered: "Alas! this dreadful thing of desire seeks its liberation in willing opposite to all my efforts of conciliation: Cannot marriage be my emancipation?"
Aaos answered: "O my sister, must thou become ever smaller from thy small desires? Oh! renounce half,desiring, much better is it to marry the evil. For thee my sister, I wish no marriage but the marriage of the greater love. For I announce, *the* day to come, yea it is nigh, *thy absorption in a male incarnation.*

What is all nature but thy past will incarnated and removed from consciousness by its further desires? The relationship still living provokes the involuntary purpose - thy opposition to which causes disease, and is but resistance of the I to the

Self.

Bind Thy desire by attention on Thy love of desire -lest it wholly runs away. Prevent thy belieffrom incarnation through this consciousness of the ever present greater desire. *Forestall* the inclinations of desire by this and not by other means of exhausting desire.

Neither abstinence nor over indulgence necessarily destroys. Verily, my sister I would have thee a male incarnation."
Then he became sleepy, his sister becoming dim and the dream more meaningless, till he felt something that made him start with horror - awaking he perceived *someone leave his couch!* Alios seizing his sword gnashing his teeth, trembling in every limb, and with ghastly visage, shouted: "Alpha and Omega! Thou thyself shall throttle that which thou wouldst surpass," And swung his sword which struck horribly ... Then shaking the perspiration from his head he muttered to himself; "Verily! again am I the pitiable moralist, the drowsiest of watchman. Sisters were ever deceivers! All virgins are foolish; What does their virginity matter?"

Then clasping his sword again he went to his couch and tried to rest but no sleep came, until daybreak: for he wondered who his sister was.

THE BUTCHER
OF THOSE
WHO FOLLOW

 N A DREAM, AAOS ONE DAY CROSSED THE BORDER LINE AND WANDERED INTO THE FLAT COUNTRY TOWARDS WHAT SEEMED, IN THE HALF~RAIN, A DESERTED HEAP OF RUINS.

Arriving closer to the city, there issued from it a dreadful stench accompanying agonizing groans. Entering the gates Aaos found it a vast slaughterer's abattoir; an endless shambles of dying bodies tied in sacks.

The black mud of the streets was streaming blood, the carnal houses bespattered, the very atmosphere pulsating agony; the grey sky reflecting its red. Holding his nose and stopping his ears Aaos walked on ... Then he paused and his frightened eyes watched the work ofslaughter and he observed that every victim was already beheaded, but not dead, that they were *sheep* and being bled to death.
As he watched the mass ofwrithing corpses in that foul Bedlam of death groans - made more loathsome by the ribald jesting of the slaughtermen, the scene became more vast, more heathenly impossible, when he noticed towering before him a giant shape with gory sheepskin used as loincloth, who, with a shrill voice shouted: "Woe unto you that seek this awful place of satiety. I am the guardian named Necrobiosis, *in order that there may be mobility!" Then* seeing Aaos he laughed hideously, and addressed him thus: "But why cometh Aaos in the *close season?* Thou old dodger of Time, thou eye winking at all things! For *thou* canst *will* love in that which is most repulsive. Away O Aaos, Thou too art an arch~slaughtererof sheep.

Then the giant gave an awful grimace and turned his back,

snapping his teeth and howling like a dog. Becoming larger and larger till of cosmic vastness, thus he disappeared. When Aaos awoke, he muttered to himself: "Beyond time there is a sensation as of awaking from the utmost impossibility of existence from the mad dreams we call reality; the stupidities we call will.

Assuredly *One would have sense minus the head*. To those awake - truths are undesirable because ever changing."

Then Aaos arose to fill his lungs with fresh air and have the good of motion.

ON THE
ANNOUNCER
OF GREAT EVENTS

 NE NIGHT, AAOS DREAMED HE WAS MOURNFULLY LABOURING HIS WAY UPHILL, THROUGH AN ENDLESS RUIN OF CITIES. THE STREETS WERE A CHAOS OF DEBRIS - THE AIR HEAVY WITH THE STALE STENCH OF DAMP CHARRED WOOD AND MOULDERING REFUSE.

Nowhere sawhe a sign oflife –
The sky was dead and breathless. Stumbling
along till his body sickened. Wearily he paused to rest and
looking down, noticed the litter of a manuscript. Stooping,
he chose the nearest fragment, and this was what he read: 'I
too was once a mighty pleasure garden of all things that
enchanted the senses; possessing men and women of every
desirable form and nationality. All the hidden treasures of
nature were exhibited with art and cunning accident. No
desire could be ungratified.... What am I now? A putrid
mess and dust of dead habitations. An empty wine skin
destroyed and gone rotten! O, stranger, what is the cause of
my de olation." Ailos, sitting down, mused long to himself:
"When the very ground beneath one's feet collapses, what is
secure? 'W'hat chance of escape - but fore-knowledge ?Would
the study of grammar or correct pronounciation of language,
save one? While he was thus meditating, suddenly he was
afraid and gave a start. For beside his shadow grew another
shadow. And when he looked round, there stood before him
an illuminated youth who said: "Awake Ailos, This sorry ruin
thou didst cause by thy greater love. All these pleasures were
but dreams, which awoke too violently. What is all sexuality
but the infinite synonyms of Self,love; self created and
destroyed? These pleasures now dead, suppressed their own
antecedent indulgence by afterthoughts of women. All

original thought, once suppressed becomes volcanic."
Alios, winking his eye, answered: "When asleep, one should
procreate in barren soil?" at which they both smiled. After
they had surveyed each other, Alios arose and left the youth.
Surmounting an eminence he searched the sky long, until he
observed the faint glow of the sun struggling through the mists,
he spake thus: "Abstinence from righteousness by total
indiscrimination, becomes limitlessness. O Sun! like thee, I
too will kiss all things and sleep alone, so that *they propagate*
my ecstasy!"

Awaking Alios remembered his *purpose,* and spoke to his heart:
"The arcana of desire *(i.e.* Self, love) would be satisfied with
none but its original Self - *by the unique.* Thus my morality
taught me by dream symbols. As in life, so in sleep - all
things have a sexual significance, hidden by righteousness.
Herein is a mystery and the *means to will.*

What is all humanity but one's own forgotten deliberation
becoming restless?

The unexpected bark of a dog should not frighten.

Neither is medicine taken by pronouncing the name of the
remedy.

Verily, in the time of cataclysm it is too late to pick the right
word."

THE DREAM

THAT CAME TRUE

 NE NIGHT AAOS WAS PLEASURED WITH THIS DREAM: IN HIS EARLY YOUTH, HE MET A BEAUTIFUL MAIDEN - FAMOUS AMONG MEN WHO KNEW PERFECTION. SHE WAS EVERYTHING DESIROUS, EVEN TO HER NAME.

He became her lover, and knew her ... to be true. But an evil voice spoke unto him and he doubted her, believing the voice - because it was of one he had made his friend. In youth-like rage he cast aside his lover and wandered into marriage of every kind, without satisfaction. Then the evil voice died. For years Aaos wandered restlessly seeking, but never finding his lost love: thinking they were both in Hell.

Then in his utmost weariness and despair, he thought much more deeply; and at last realized that the dream was the time for magic. And then he willed ... With the new moon his wish was materialized and again he met his first and only love. Their hearts being still virgin, Aaos spoke unto her: "Out of Chaos have I awaked and found thee, O beloved. Death itself shall not part us; for by thee alone will I have children." And they married *and were ecstatic thereafter:* for in their ecstasy he noticed Death smile.

Aaos then awoke still living their ecstasy, and breathing heavily, spake to himself thus: "When the thing *desired* is again incarnated at the time of ecstasy; there can be no satiety. ONE! we now part.

All things are possible with the original belief, once again found.

The belief, simultaneous with the desire, becomes its parallel and duality ceases.

When ecstasy is transcended by ecstasy, the *I* becomes atmospheric - there is no place for sensuous objects to conceive *differently* and react.

Verily, greater will has no man than to - jest in ecstasy: retain thyself from giving forth thy seed of life."

Aaos rising from his couch - threw away his sword and exclaimed aloud:

"NOW FOR REALITY!"

CPSIA information can be obtained at www.ICGtesting.com
Printed in the USA
BVIW12n1106140417
481227BV00018B/56